WHAT'S happening TO ME?

Alex Frith and Micaela Tapsell
Illustrated by Sr. Sanchez

Designed by: Neil Francis

WITH EXPERT ADVICE FROM:
Laura Clarke, sex educator
Dr Anna Forringer-Beal, gender studies researcher
Dr Caitríona Cox, medical doctor

CONTENTS

GROWING UP	3
WHEN WILL PUBERTY BEGIN?	4
TALLER AND DEEPER	8
GETTING HAIRY	10
BETWEEN YOUR LEGS	14
YOU AND YOUR GENDER	20
WHAT HAPPENS TO GIRLS?	24
GROWING BREASTS	28
HAVING CRUSHES	30
YOUR BODY, YOUR RULES	32
WHAT ACTUALLY IS SEX?	34
SAFE SEX	36
SEX ON THE INTERNET	38
LOOKING AFTER YOU	40
OLDER AND WISER	50
YOUR SUPPORT CREW	52
TOO GOOD TO BE TRUE?	56
BECOMING YOU	58
GLOSSARY	60
INDEX	62
ACKNOWLEDGEMENTS	64

GROWING UP

You've been growing up little by little ever since you were born, but there's a time when you'll start to change a lot. That's when you begin to grow from a child into an adult, and it's what this book is all about.

You might have noticed some changes happening to you and your friends already, or maybe there haven't been any yet.

They don't happen to everyone at the same age, or in the same way, and you can't tell in advance when they'll happen to you. But this book will give you a good idea of what to expect.

This new phase in your life is called puberty. It's all to do with growing up and preparing your body for being a grown-up. Perhaps you're looking forward to growing up, or maybe you have doubts. Don't worry – the changes take place gradually, so you'll have plenty of time to get used to them.

WHEN WILL PUBERTY BEGIN?

People usually say boys start changing at 12 or 13, but it happens to some people earlier than this and to others quite a bit later. The fact is, when your body is ready, you'll start growing up.

YOUR WEIGHT

First of all, you have to build up some fat. This is a healthy way for your body to store the energy it needs for the changes ahead.

Everyone grows up at their own pace. You might be the same age as your friends, but you could finish developing before they start, or the other way around.

You can't make yourself grow up faster, or more slowly. But one thing's for sure – everyone gets to the same stage in the end. No matter how old you are when you start puberty, you'll go on changing until you're fully grown up.

WHAT NEXT?

Just so you know what to expect, here are some growing-up changes you'll be likely to experience — if you haven't already. Don't worry if you don't recognize some of these words — they'll all be explained later in the book.

- Your pubic hair starts to grow.
- Hair grows under your arms, and maybe on your chest and back.
- You start to sweat more.
- Your skin and hair may get greasier.
- Your testicles get bigger, and start making something called sperm.
- Your penis gets bigger, and gets stiff sometimes.
- You get taller, broader and heavier.
- Your voice gets deeper.

It can take a few years from the very first changes of puberty to the last. And it will be several more years after that before you finish growing up. All along, you'll start to feel a bit different in yourself. Don't worry though; you'll still be you at the end of it all — just a more grown-up version of yourself.

HOW DOES IT START?

To get puberty started, your body needs chemical messengers called sex hormones. Before it can make them, it needs a signal from different parts of your brain. It works like this...

LOCATION: HYPOTHALAMUS, BRAIN.

I'm a hormone called GnRH. I've got a message to send from my part of the brain to another part...

LOCATION: PITUITARY GLAND, BRAIN

GnRH says it's time to start making two new hormones: FSH and LH. Send them to the testicles.

TESTICLES WORKSHOP

Hello! Word from the brain is, please can you start making sex hormones. And start making sperm, too, while you're at it.

BALLS OF ACTIVITY

You won't *feel* anything, but as puberty hits, your testicles – or balls – are hard at work. They create millions of sperm every day. To do this, they have to be at a temperature just a little lower than your body – which is why your balls hang below your belly, not inside your body.

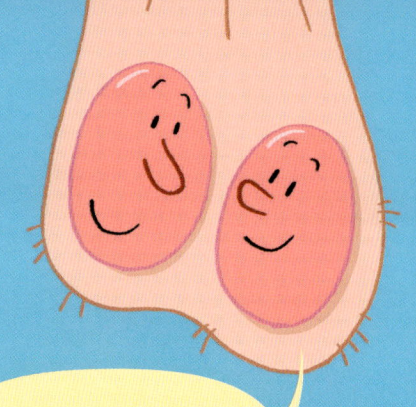

I'm a little lower than you – so we don't knock into each other. No pain, please!

Testicles also make sex hormones, which tell your body to grow and develop in all sorts of ways. You might've heard of testosterone, which plays a part in this. But there are lots of other ones, for example oestrogen and progesterone. Everyone has all these hormones, although male bodies tend to have more testosterone than female ones.

FEELING EMOTIONAL

You need hormones to tell your body what to do. But, when lots of hormones are bossing it around all at once, it can get to be a bit MUCH. During puberty, it's normal to feel moody, tearful or more sensitive than usual, and for you not really to know why.

Don't worry! As you grow, your hormones – and your emotions – will settle down.

TALLER AND DEEPER

When everyone starts telling you how much you've grown, the chances are that other changes are on the way too. Once you're a little taller, you'll probably start broadening out as well. Not everyone has a really obvious growth spurt. Some seem to grow more gradually over several years.

A GROWTH SPURT

Boys usually grow fastest around the time they're 14, but you may grow tall when you're quite a bit younger or older than this. Some boys keep on growing into their early 20s.

If you go through a growth spurt early, it's likely that you'll stop growing early too. And if you start later, you may well catch up with the early growers and even overtake them.

Growing taller also means getting heavier – because your bones, muscles and organs all weigh more as they get bigger. It's normal to double in weight from age 10 to age 18.

BIGGER MUSCLES, DEEPER VOICE

All your muscles get bigger during puberty, including the ones you can't see – such as your heart and lungs. Your voice box, which sits in your neck, also grows bigger and thicker. This will make your voice deeper over time.

Some boys find their voice box sticks out as a small bump on their necks. It's so common it has a nickname – an Adam's Apple. Yours might show, or it might not.

Adam's apple

It takes time to learn to control your voice box as it changes shape. This is not something to worry about, but it does means two things.

1) Sometimes, your words will come out sounding squeaky or weird, because the muscles in your voice box aren't quite doing what you want them to yet.

2) Your voice at 16 will probably sound a lot different than it did at 12. People might tell you that your voice has "broken". They don't mean it literally – it's just a different, deeper sound.

Hey mate, long time no see.

Crikey! You sound like a grown-up.

GETTING HAIRY

During puberty, you'll start getting hair in places you didn't have it before. The hair is natural and everybody gets it.

PUBIC HAIR

Pubic hair can grow around your genitals, on your lower stomach, inner thighs and between your bum cheeks. It gets more curly as it grows, and might be a different colour from the hair on your head.

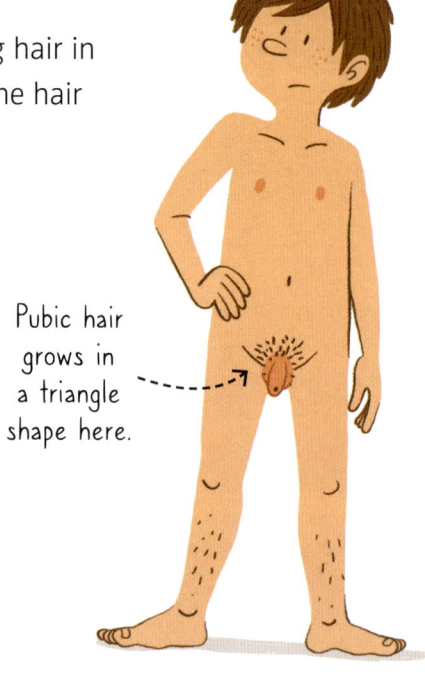

Pubic hair grows in a triangle shape here.

ALL OVER YOUR BODY

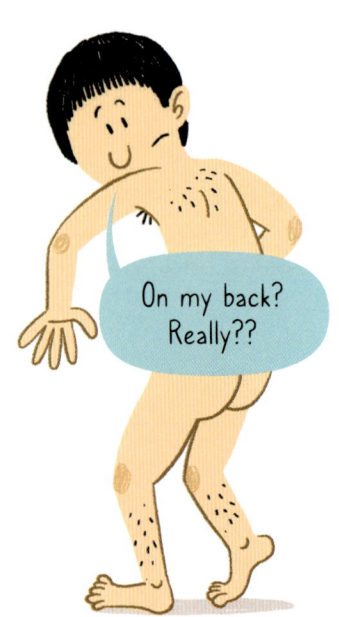

On my back? Really??

It's normal to get thicker hair on other parts of your body, too. You might notice it on your arms and legs, your chest, maybe on the backs of your hands and the tops of your feet. Some people keep all their body hair; others shave some or even all of it.

Throughout your life you may well keep on getting hairier. Hair may grow on your chest, your shoulders and back, although it's hard to see it there without a mirror. But this isn't true for everyone – some boys find they grow very little extra hair, or perhaps none at all.

UNDER YOUR ARMS

About a year after you get pubic hair, you'll notice hair starts growing in your armpits, too. You might also find more people your age using underarm deodorant – a roll-on liquid or spray that hides body smells.

The hair doesn't make your armpits smell. But the hair can trap sweat from under your arms, and that can start to smell if it soaks into your clothes. Sweating is totally normal, and puberty tends to make you sweat more. Keep clean – and use the deodorant.

WHAT'S THE HAIR FOR?

No one really knows why people get pubic and armpit hair. It may be precisely because it gives sweat something to cling to.

Many animals use their sweaty smell to attract a mate, but scientists are still debating whether this works for humans.

HAIR UP THERE

There's one other place where many boys grow new hair: their faces. Often it's noticeable on the upper lip before anywhere else.

Some full-grown men grow facial hair fast enough that they need to shave it every day. Others prefer to grow it and sculpt it in different ways.

Hair just on your upper lip is called a moustache.

Hair growing on and under your chin is a beard.

Patches of hair next to your ears are called sideburns.

Shaving and letting the beard grow a little bit creates stubble.

Hair in a small triangle under your lips is called a soul patch.

Whichever option you choose, you do need to take care of your face. It's a good idea to use moisturizing lotion after shaving.

IS IT ONLY BOYS THAT GROW BEARDS?

Growing hair isn't anything to do with being a boy or a girl. All humans are mammals, and that means almost all of us have a fine covering of hair all over our bodies.

During puberty, no matter your sex, you'll find some of those hairs get longer, thicker and, usually, darker. Everyone grows pubic hair and armpit hair. Almost everyone notices thicker hair on their arms, legs and upper lip. Most males grow noticeable facial hair. Whether a person shaves their face or body hair, or lets it grow, it's a personal choice.

While we're talking about different sexes, it's worth pointing out that LOTS of puberty changes are the same for girls too. Such as...

There are SOME things that happen to female bodies that don't happen to male ones. You can read about those things on pages 24-29.

BETWEEN YOUR LEGS

A change you'll definitely notice during puberty is that your private parts get bigger. You won't notice it day to day, but your penis and testicles will grow quite a bit. Before talking more about what happens and why, it's helpful to label the parts we're talking about in detail.

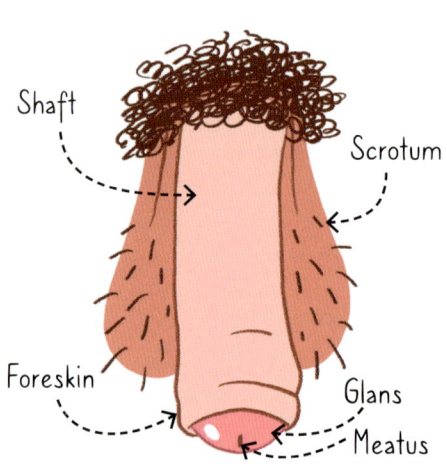

Your bits on the outside

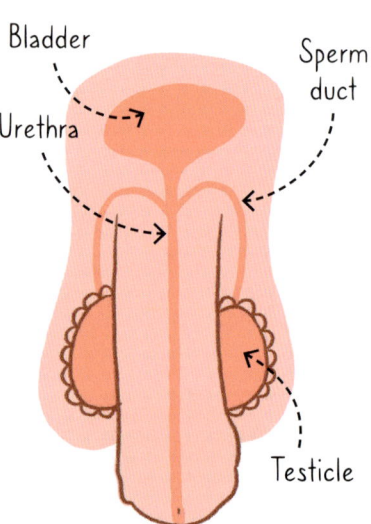

Your bits on the inside

WHERE'S MY FORESKIN?

You may or may not have a foreskin. It's a fold of skin that covers the head of your penis. In some countries, it's common for a doctor to cut it off soon after birth, or around the time puberty starts – often for religious reasons. It doesn't matter if you have one or not, it just means your penis might look different from some other boys'.

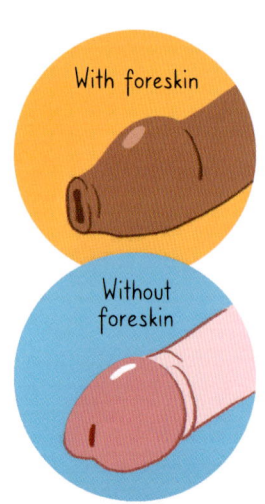

14

HOW BIG DOES IT GET?

As you might already realize, measuring a penis is not straightforward. Penises seem to change size all the time, during the course of each day. When you're cold, your balls get pulled up closer to your belly to keep them warm. Often, the skin around your penis shrivels too, making it look smaller.

If you have a big belly, you might find that some of your penis is tucked up inside. It doesn't mean you have a smaller penis than other boys, just that less of it is visible when it's floppy.

Inside your penis there's lots of spongy tissue that's designed to fill up with blood, but not all the time. You'll know when it's full of blood, because this makes your penis get a lot longer, turns it stiff, and makes it point forward or stick up. This is called having an erection.

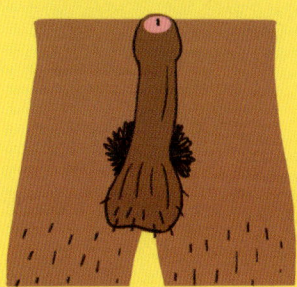

Some erections are straight; others bend to one side.

If you have a foreskin, this might get pulled back, or might not.

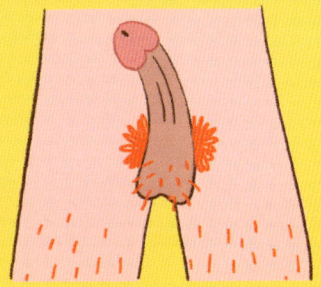

ALL ABOUT ERECTIONS

Erections can happen at any time, but most commonly happen if you touch or play with your penis. This is usually a nice feeling. You may have had erections as long as you can remember, or may never have had one. You may find you don't get them until you hit puberty.

Playing with your penis – called masturbation – is very common. It's your private time to explore your body, behind closed doors. Sometimes, playing with yourself builds up to a shaking, shuddering, happy feeling called an orgasm – also known as "coming". Most people only experience this for the first time after puberty begins. Typically, as an orgasm happens, your penis will squirt out a little bit – around a teaspoonful – of whitish goo called semen. This is a mixture of sperm and liquid that the sperm swims in. It's made in your testicles and some other body bits hiding behind your penis.

That's new.

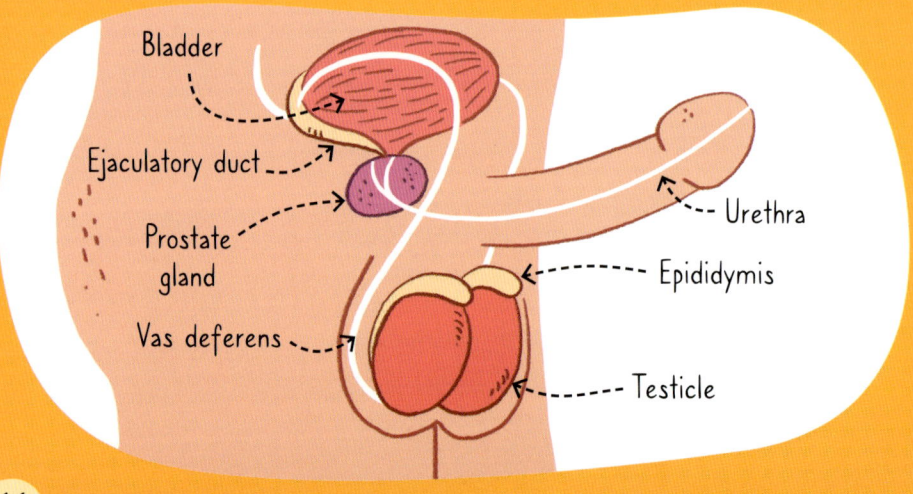

When semen comes out, it's called ejaculating. Sometimes, it spurts out a little distance; other times it just oozes out. It's wet, so might leave a patch on your clothes, but it washes out easily. You can usually clean it up with a couple of tissues or even a sock.

After ejaculating, your erection will go down pretty quickly, and your penis won't be able to get hard again for a little while. Some time later, you'll probably want to go to the toilet – this is your body's way of cleaning out the inside of your penis.

Masturbating isn't just something boys do – it's very common whatever your gender, and whatever genitals you have. Some people never do it, but others do it every day. Even if you don't want to masturbate, or never feel the urge, it's very normal to explore your genitals with your hands. But if you do, do it behind closed doors!

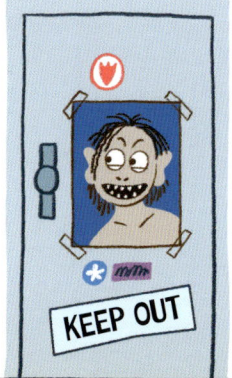

NIGHT AND DAY

Lots of boys experience an ejaculation for the first time while they're asleep. It's often the end part of a dream called a wet dream. Some have these dreams almost every night; others have them occasionally or not at all. The dream itself may or may not have anything to do with sex; there's no special meaning to them.

Even if you never have a wet dream, you might well wake up some mornings with an erection. This is perfectly normal. It's also very common, especially when you're a teenager, to find you get erections with no warning throughout the day, even when you wish you didn't have one.

Erections usually go away after just a few minutes, especially if you can find a way to distract yourself from thinking about it. But you might want to keep a bag or coat or something handy you can use to cover the telltale bulge.

If you're surrounded by other people and want to get rid of an erection, you can try distracting yourself by listing some really boring facts in your head...

1x7 = 7
2x7 = 14
3x7 = 21
4x7 = 28
5x7 = 35
6x7 = 42
7x7 = 49
8x7 = ??

50 States of America
Wives of Henry VIII
Names for all the dinosaurs

GOOD TO KNOW

Your body is designed so you can't ejaculate and pee at the same time. This makes it hard to pee when you have an erection. But it is possible, and peeing while you have an erection is one way to make it start to go down.

YOU AND YOUR GENDER

Everyone changes as they grow, but the way you look on the outside is only part of the process. How you feel inside your head is really important too. It's partly to do with something called gender, and something else called sex. They're two different things.

YOUR BITS DOWN THERE

Your sex depends on the body bits you were born with. Most people are either male – with a penis – or female – with a vulva. When you were born, it's likely that a doctor looked at your genitals and said "It's a girl!" or "It's a boy!" But there's more to it than that.

Gender is different from sex because it's all about how you feel, rather than what body parts you have. You may feel like a boy, a girl, both or neither.

You might feel differently about your gender over time. It isn't a fixed thing; it can shift and change as you grow through puberty and into adulthood.

LABELS

Some people find it helpful to label the way their sex and gender do or don't line up. If your gender matches your sex, you are *cisgender*.

If your gender doesn't match the body parts you were born with, then you might be *transgender* or *non-binary*.

There are labels for your sex, too. Roughly two out of every one hundred people are born with a mix of male AND female body parts. The technical name for this is being *intersex*. You often can't tell just by looking. For example, if you have male genitals on the outside, but female genitals on the inside, you might not have any idea of being intersex until you hit puberty.

If you are intersex, it's common to start puberty later, and experience some changes but not others, depending on the hormones swirling around inside you.

GENDER STEREOTYPES

It's pretty common, especially for grown-ups, to have ideas about what makes girls and boys different. This might be about what sorts of things one gender "ought to" like, or how another gender "ought to" behave. These are stereotypes, and they're often WRONG. Here are some examples of typical stereotypes about boys and girls.

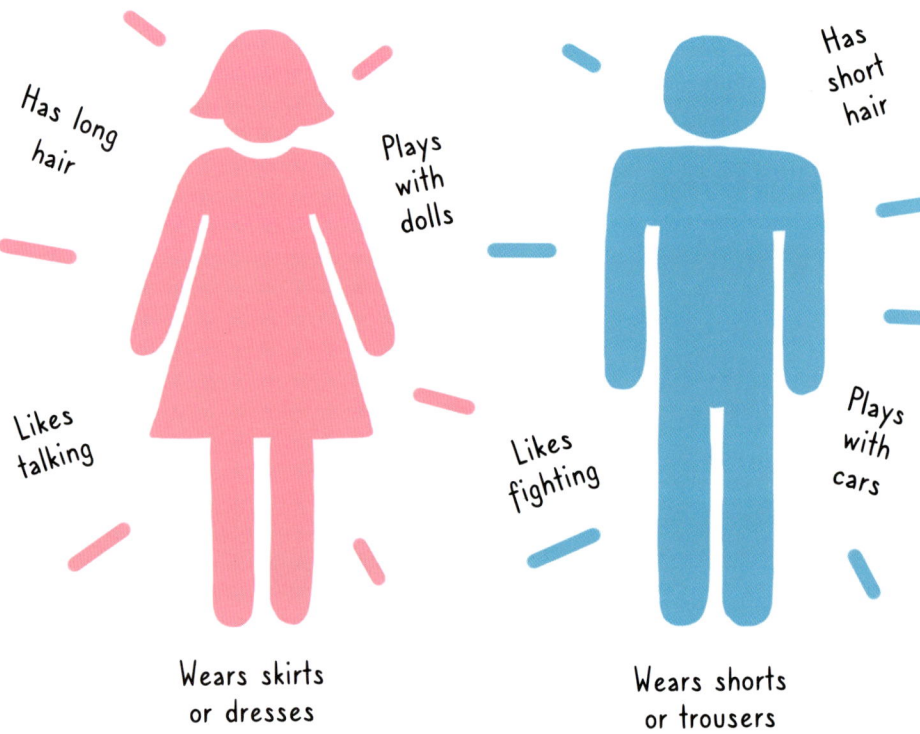

Some people do look and act in ways that fit a stereotype, but just as many people don't. The chances are, you feel SOME of the stereotypes about your sex match the way you think about yourself, but lots of them don't, no matter whether you are cis or trans or non-binary.

BEING YOURSELF

As you get older, you might start to feel pressure to be less childish and to act more like a grown-up. That sometimes includes people telling you to look and behave more like the gender THEY think is appropriate for your sex.

It can be tough if you don't want to do, dress or act how other people think you should. The fact is, there are many ways to be a boy or a girl – too many to make rules about. Equally, if you feel like your sex doesn't match your gender, there are no rules about how you should look or act or dress to express your gender identity. It's enough just to be yourself.

WHAT HAPPENS TO GIRLS?

Everyone goes through lots of growing up changes during puberty, no matter their gender. Female bodies typically start puberty sooner than male ones, and they go through several changes male bodies don't. But mentally, everyone will feel a similar swirl of confusion, excitement, embarrassment and mixed emotions.

GIRL PARTS

Some of the biggest changes that girls experience are about their private parts, on the outside and the inside. The parts on the outside are known together as the *vulva*.

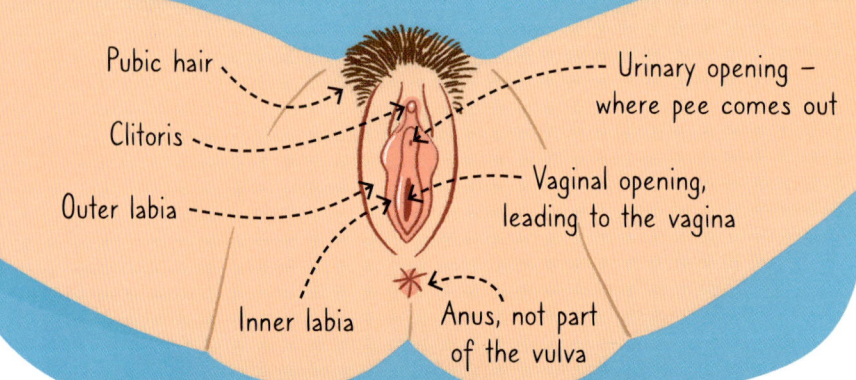

ALL KINDS ARE NORMAL

As much as penises vary, so do vulvas; there's no "correct" way for a vulva to look. Likewise, pubic hair can grow around a vulva in different patterns and thickness. Here are just a few examples.

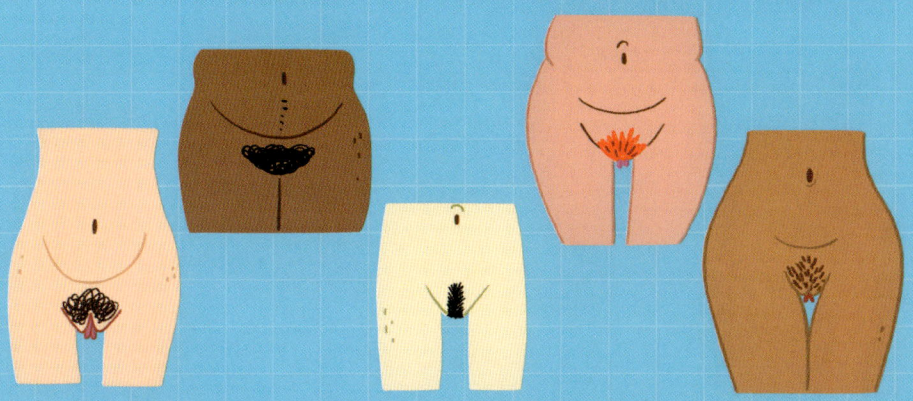

The vulva is made up of different parts, including two thick folds of skin called the outer labia (lips). Inside the outer labia are two smaller lips called the inner labia. These may be different lengths from each other, and sometimes stick out. At the front, where the inner labia meet, is a pea-shaped bump called the clitoris. The clitoris and labia are sensitive to touch — just like the head of a penis.

Vulvas can swell up with blood, and a clitoris can stiffen, in a similar way to an erection. This often happens when masturbating. This may also make the vagina produce a slippery fluid, and can lead to an orgasm.

The vagina is a squishy tube that goes a few inches inside the body. Its opening can stretch, and may be surrounded by a thin layer of skin called the hymen. The hymen usually wears away over time. The vagina is part of the body that cleans itself, thanks to a clear, slightly sticky fluid, called discharge.

MONTHLY CYCLE

One BIG experience female bodies have that male ones don't is something called a "period". This is when a small amount of blood and other bits come out of the vagina over the course of a few days, roughly once every month. It happens because of changes going on inside a female body.

Here are the main parts involved:

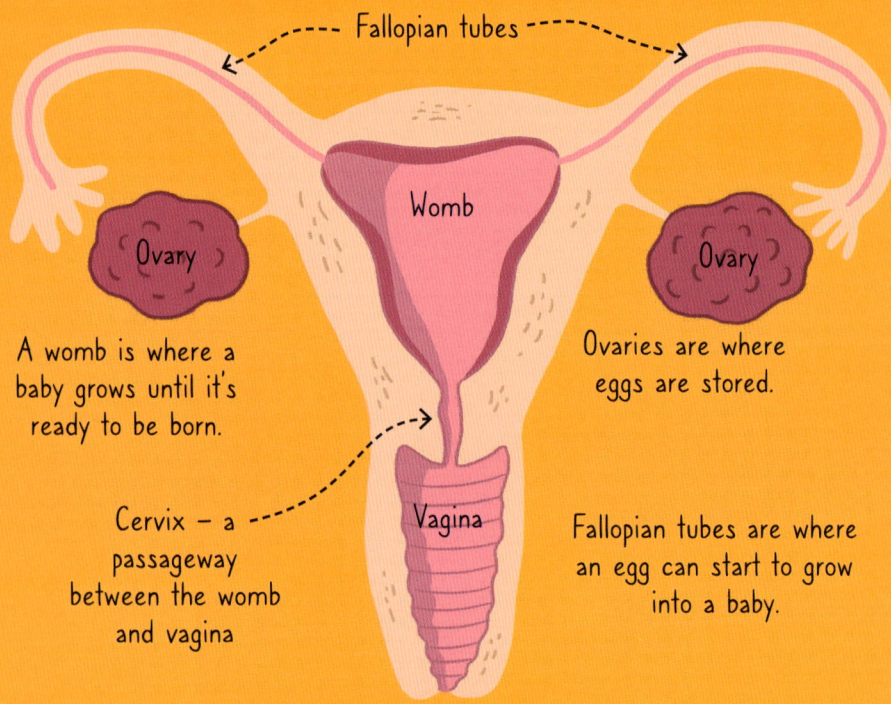

A womb is where a baby grows until it's ready to be born.

Ovaries are where eggs are stored.

Cervix – a passageway between the womb and vagina

Fallopian tubes are where an egg can start to grow into a baby.

During puberty, a series of hormone messages inside a female body tell the ovaries to start releasing one egg, roughly once each month. Usually, after a few weeks, the egg comes out of the vagina, along with a thin layer of the womb – its lining – and some blood. This mixture is what makes up a period.

WHAT'S A PERIOD LIKE?

Sometimes it's a light period, which means only a little blood comes out of the vagina. Sometimes it's a heavy period, which means quite a lot of blood comes out. The average is six tablespoons of blood. Most girls buy and carry around things called period products to soak up that blood.
These include...

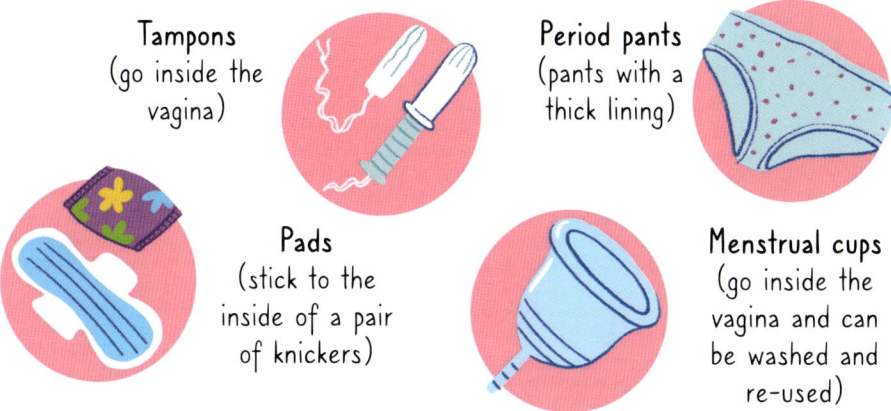

Tampons
(go inside the vagina)

Period pants
(pants with a thick lining)

Pads
(stick to the inside of a pair of knickers)

Menstrual cups
(go inside the vagina and can be washed and re-used)

Periods aren't just about bleeding for a few days. They're painful, too, caused by the feeling of a womb tightening. Sometimes, having a period can be so painful that only lying down, a hot water bottle or pain killers can relieve it.

Often in the days before a period starts, girls experience something known as PMS – premenstrual syndrome. This is when hormones cause tiredness, irritation, headaches, anger, anxiety or sadness.

People feel all kinds of ways about their periods. Some find them really annoying and very painful, others don't care much, and some even feel energetic after. It's never helpful or kind to point out that someone is on their period, so don't do it.

GROWING BREASTS

Did you know, around half of all boys find they develop breasts? Typically, they swell up just a little, but usually reduce in size a few months or years later.

Almost all girls develop them. Some find they can feel a bit sore, tingly or itchy as they grow. One breast may grow faster than the other, but they'll even out eventually – although no one has exactly symmetrical breasts. They continue to change when you're a grown-up too.

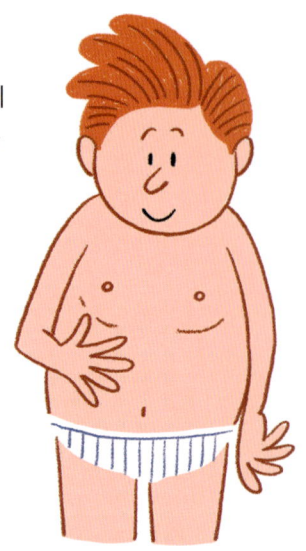

The shape and size of breasts, and nipples, differs from person to person. ALL of them are normal.

BREASTS AND MILK

Breasts are able to make milk – but only after a baby is born. It comes out of the nipples through tiny holes. Breasts are mostly made of fat, which cushions the milk-making parts.

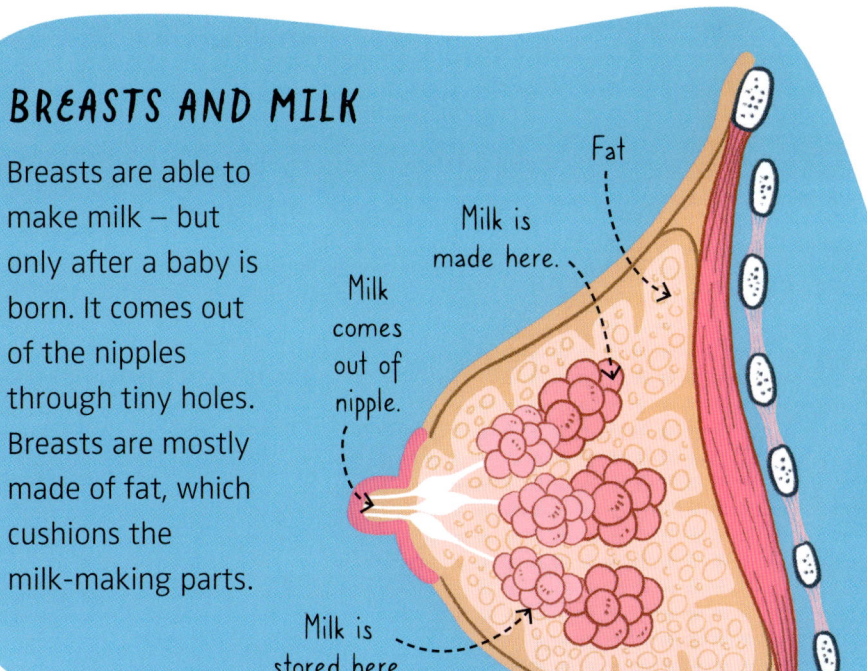

Fat

Milk is made here.

Milk comes out of nipple.

Milk is stored here.

BRA BUSINESS

Some girls wear a bra to support their breasts and backs. There are bras for all different sizes, big and small, and they all come in a variety of styles, such as...

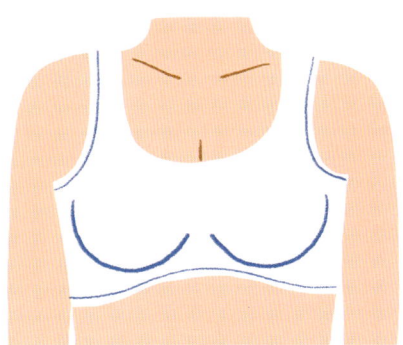

...a sports bra, that holds breasts in position and keeps them cool during exercise.

...a smooth bra, without lots of seams and decoration. This is often called a T-shirt bra.

HAVING CRUSHES

You'll probably start to think in new ways as you get older. For example, you might start to have crushes on people. This means a mix of things, such as thinking they're good-looking, or wanting to be around them, and hoping that they like *you*.

It's normal to feel excited or nervous when your crush is near. Having crushes is part of something called your sexuality, even though it's not always to do with sex. Some people find it helpful to give their sexuality a name – here are some examples.

BISEXUAL (Bi)
Attracted to people of more than one gender.

HETEROSEXUAL
Boys who are only attracted to girls, and girls who are only attracted to boys. Also known as being "straight".

PANSEXUAL
Attracted to other people, regardless of their gender, sex or sexuality.

HOMOSEXUAL
Attracted to people who are of the same sex or gender. Also known as being "gay". Gay girls often call themselves lesbians.

ASEXUAL
Not sexually attracted to anyone, but may or may not still feel romantically attracted to other people.

QUESTIONING
Someone who is questioning their sexuality, or curious about exploring other sexualities.

COMING OUT

People often wrongly assume that everyone is straight, unless they're told otherwise. Someone who isn't straight might choose to tell other people about their sexuality. This is known as "coming out". It's a personal decision if, when, and how you choose to do it.

Some people are certain about their sexuality from a very young age, while other people discover more about themselves and get a better understanding of it over time. You can't choose your sexuality – it's just the way you are, and part of what makes you YOU.

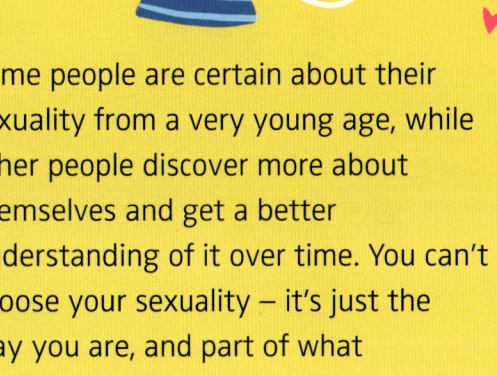

As you grow up, it's natural to have questions about romance and sex, and even to wonder what it might be like to touch another person's private body bits. But before you explore your feelings with someone else, you must ask for consent first. That's what the next page is all about.

YOUR BODY, YOUR RULES

Your body belongs to YOU. This means nobody else can decide what you do with it. Before somebody touches you, they must ask for your permission. The same goes if you want to touch someone – this is called asking for consent.

Everyone is comfortable with different things, and it's important that we respect each other's boundaries. You can do this by asking if someone minds before you enter their personal space. Here are some examples of what this might look like:

THE RIGHT TO SAY NO

When someone asks YOU for consent, you can say yes, no or change your mind. You also don't need to give a reason – no means no. It's not okay for someone to pressure you into saying yes, or make you feel bad for saying no. And if you change your mind, they have to respect your decision.

If you feel worried, unsure or scared, try telling the person to stop, or move away – and tell someone else what happened. Nobody, adult or child, has the right to make you feel bad in your own body.

CONSENT AND SEX

Sometimes people touch each other's private body bits. This is a different, more grown-up type of touching, and both people need to give permission first. It's against the law to touch anybody's penis, vulva, breasts or bottom without their permission. If anyone touches yours, or makes you touch theirs, it's not your fault and you should tell an adult.

You might be curious to know what this grown-up touching is all about, so turn the page to find out...

WHAT ACTUALLY IS SEX?

Sex is when grown-ups touch the sensitive parts of each other's genitals in a way that might lead to an orgasm. This happens between people of all genders and for lots of different reasons. People have sex to show love and affection for each other – and because it feels good.

BABY-MAKING SEX

People might also have sex in order to make a baby. This type of sex involves a penis and a vagina.
It typically happens like this...

First, a couple kiss and cuddle each other closely. This is called foreplay, and it gets their bodies ready to have sex. The penis becomes erect and the vagina enlarges, and releases some slippery fluid which helps the penis fit inside it. Both people move around, making the inside of the vagina rub against the outside of the penis. The penis ejaculates semen. The semen contains many millions of sperm, which are tiny cells that swim up through the vagina. If they meet an egg in the fallopian tubes, one of the sperm could join with it...

...and a baby may start growing.

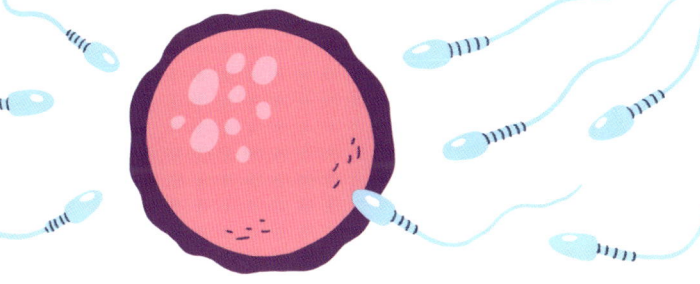

JUST FOR FUN

The idea of playing with other people's bits might seem really weird. But lots of adults really like doing it, and one change that affects many teens during puberty is finding they want to do it, too. It's a common part of grown-up relationships. But in most places, it's against the law to have sex before the age of 16. This is known as the "Age of Consent".

SAFE SEX

Sex comes with risks. One of those risks is getting pregnant, even if you don't want to. Another is catching or spreading disease. People can have sex with less risk of pregnancy using something called contraception. To prevent spreading diseases, they use things called prophylactics. There are several types.

One type that works as contraception AND as a prophylactic is a condom. This is a thin rubber cover that goes over the penis before it enters the vagina. The end of the condom has a small bump which catches semen and stops the sperm from reaching the egg.

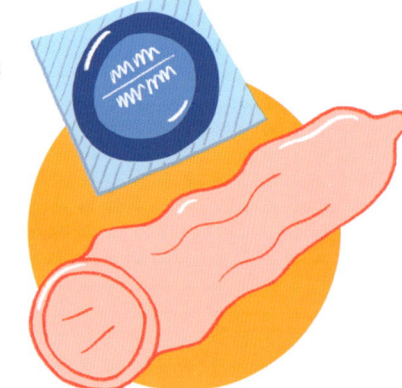

A condom comes in a wrapper, and can be unrolled onto an erect penis.

The contraceptive pill

Another method of contraception *only* is a kind of pill, usually prescribed by a doctor. It affects the female hormone cycle, and it's quite common for some girls to take it to help ease bad acne, or very heavy periods. It's used by so many people, it's often known simply as "the pill".

There are other methods of contraception and they all do a good job at preventing pregnancy, but no method is guaranteed to work every time.

SEX MYTHS

As you get older, you might notice that people start to talk about sex more and more. The chances are that some of what you hear isn't exactly true, especially when it comes to safe sex. Despite what people might tell you, a person CAN get pregnant...

...even if it's their first time having sex.

...if the penis pulls out of the vagina before it ejaculates.

...even if you do it standing up.

...even if the penis doesn't go all the way in.

The only way to have safe sex is to use contraception.

AVOIDING INFECTIONS

There are some infections that people can spread or catch when they have sex. These are called sexually transmitted infections, or STIs. To prevent STIs, people can use a type of contraception that covers their private body bits, such as a condom. This acts as a barrier that blocks infections from passing between people during sex.

SEX ON THE INTERNET

At some point, you might come across videos or photos of people having sex or doing sexual things. This is called pornography, or porn, and it's a type of entertainment that is created ONLY for adults. Lots of young people are exposed to porn through the internet, long before they are ready to understand it.

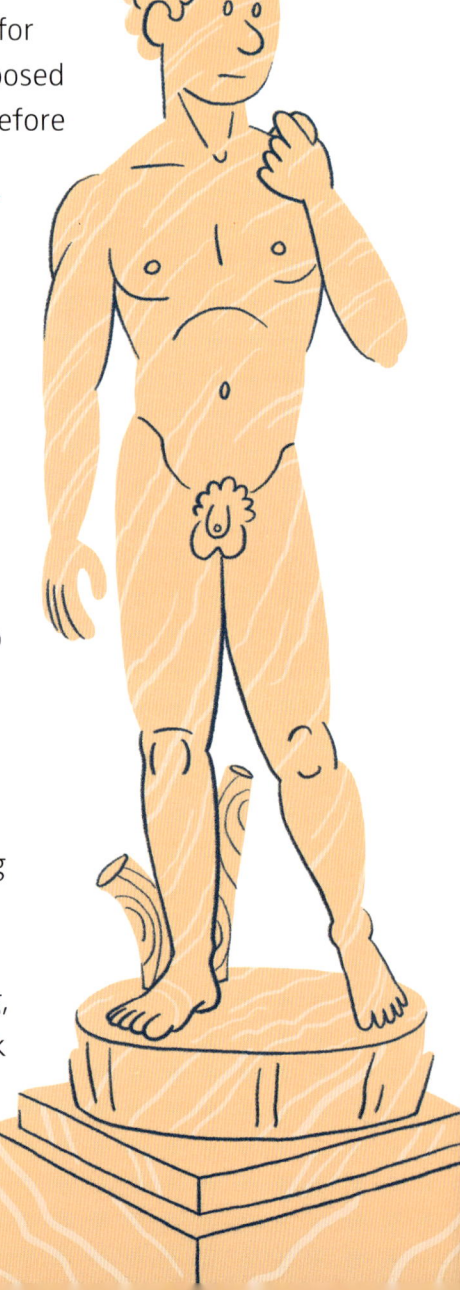

> Not all naked pictures online are pornographic – they might be scientific diagrams, paintings or ancient statues, like me!

Most countries have laws in place to restrict porn for people under a certain age (usually around 18). Parents, schools or companies can use filters to block it online, but some can still sneak through. Seeing porn might make you feel very uncomfortable, upset or scared. These feelings can be overwhelming, so you might find it helpful to speak to an adult you trust.

DON'T BELIEVE EVERYTHING YOU SEE

Most porn doesn't reflect what regular people look like, or how they act during sex. After all, people in porn are *performing* sex, as actors. They do everything in a way that's easy for a camera to see, and it's often all planned out. They don't show what real sex looks like, and they're not role models for how you or anyone else is supposed to look or act during sex.

Looking at porn doesn't mean you're weird or a bad person. It's natural to be curious. But it's also completely normal if you haven't seen it, or don't want to see it. If a friend shows you porn, it's okay to feel embarrassed or overwhelmed. You can ask them to switch it off, or move away.

LOOKING AFTER YOU

Adults often tease teenagers for being selfish, and not thinking about other people. In fact, everyone can be selfish at times. There are good reasons why you SHOULD think about yourself and your needs, especially when you're going through puberty.

That usually means spending a bit of time on your own, relaxing, de-stressing and hiding away from the world.

For a lot of people, taking this time regularly is enough to stay on top of their mental health. Your mental health is about your thoughts and feelings. Everyone has times when they feel a little worried, or sad – even quite deeply – from time to time.

TIPS FOR DE-STRESSING

There are plenty of ways to unwind from life's stresses and worries, if you can find the time and space to do them. You could try...

ASKING FOR HELP

If your worries become overwhelming, or are making it hard for you to relax, it's really important that you TALK to someone – perhaps a parent or friend or teacher. If worries are seriously affecting your life, it can be a good idea to see your doctor.

FUELLING YOUR BODY

Eating a balanced diet will give you all the nutrients you need to feel healthy and energetic during the ups and downs of puberty. There are lots of different types of food and each has an important job to do.

Carbohydrates
These give you long-lasting energy.

Fruit and vegetables
These give you essential vitamins, minerals and fibre, which help protect you from diseases and keep your digestive system working properly.

Proteins
These help your body grow and repair itself.

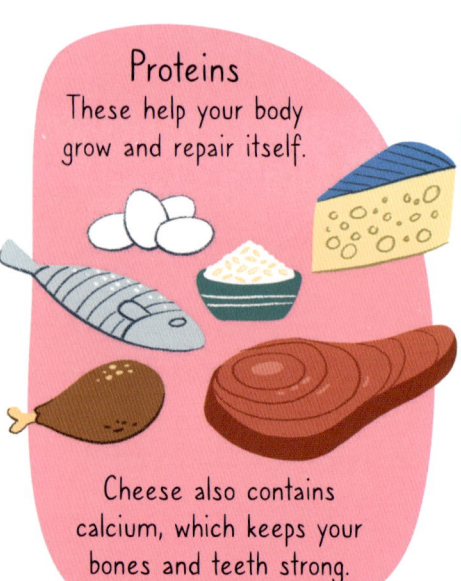

Cheese also contains calcium, which keeps your bones and teeth strong.

Fats
Fat keeps your skin and hair and guts healthy.

Water
Drinking water keeps your body hydrated so that it can function properly.

HOW MUCH?

During puberty, you need as much food – or more – than an adult because you're growing so fast. So eat when you feel hungry – it's your body's way of storing energy for the changes ahead.

BREAKFAST

Try to make time for breakfast. Your body uses energy even while you're asleep and you need to replace it in the morning. A healthy breakfast stops you feeling weak and sluggish, improves your concentration and helps you function better all round.

FOOD AND TEETH

Most of your adult teeth will probably have come through by the age of 13, and they will last you for life. To keep your teeth and gums healthy, you need to brush twice a day. If you have braces, it's a good idea to use interdental brushes to clean properly around each tooth.

Angle your brush like this to clean the back of your teeth.

KEEP MOVING

Exercise is really good for your physical and mental health. It helps you to sleep well and feel more energetic. It also keeps your heart and bones healthy, which is especially important during puberty when your body is changing. There are LOTS of different ways to get exercise, so try to find something you enjoy. This could be…

…anything you like!

HOW MUCH?

If you can, you should try to exercise for at least 150 minutes (2½ hours) a week. This sounds like a lot but it can be split into 10 minute bouts and can include walking to school. Exercise doesn't have to be very tiring; you just need to get your heart beating faster than normal for a few minutes.

Soku-TOH!

When you exercise, your brain produces lots of feel-good hormones called endorphins. They help you to feel more positive and confident, and can reduce pain, stress and anxiety. This is why people usually feel really good after exercising.

REST AND SLEEP

Puberty is hard work for your body and your brain, so you need time to rest and recover. While you're asleep, your body repairs itself, and your dreams may help you to learn and make sense of things that have happened to you. It's also an important part of looking after your mental health, so aim to get around 10 hours of sleep each night.

KEEP CLEAN

You'll need to wash a bit more now than you did when you were younger. This is because you start to sweat more. You have sweat glands all over your skin, but there are more in some areas, such as your armpits and around your genitals. It's a good idea to wash those bits every day, even if it's just with a wet flannel or sponge.

Keeping clean doesn't just mean bathing or showering – you have to keep your clothes clean, too. Any clothes close to your skin – such as socks, pants and T-shirts – are likely to pick up sweat, and the bacteria that loves sweat. You might want to wash those items after each day of wearing them.

Want to learn how to do this for yourself? It's easy!

You probably won't notice if your clothes smell bad while you're wearing them. But if you do a smell test after you've taken them off, it'll help you work out when it's time to put them in the laundry. One day before too long, it'll be *you* doing the laundry, anyway...

CLEANING DOWN THERE

If you have a foreskin, as you grow older you need to start keeping this clean, on the inside as well as the outside.

But don't start too soon! Before puberty, your foreskin is likely stuck to the head of the penis. As you get older, it starts to loosen. In time you should be able to roll it all the way back, although this may take until you're 18. You may not be able to do this much when you have an erection – this is normal, and it won't affect how your penis works.

Beneath your foreskin, bits of dead skin and body oils can build up and form small whitish flakes, called smegma. This is totally normal, and you can wash it away with water. Don't use soap, as it's likely to make the tip of your penis itchy.

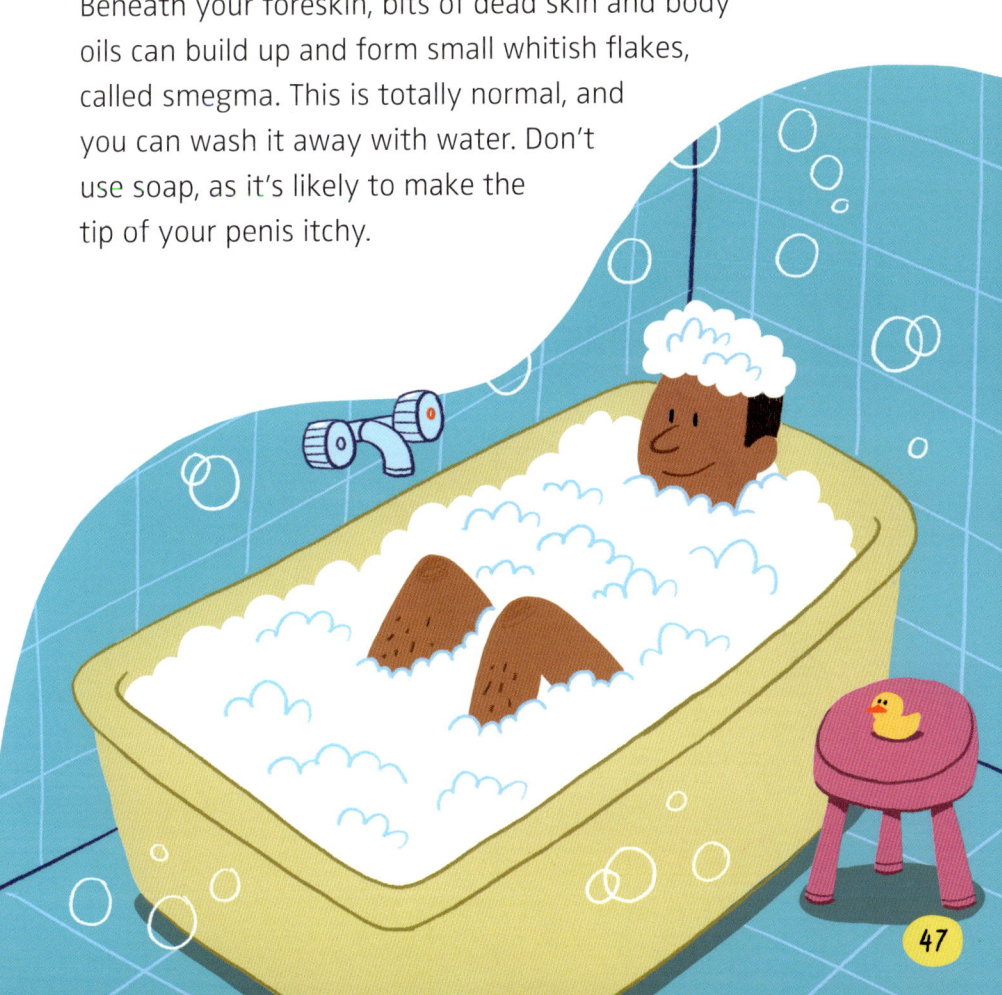

FROM THE NECK UP

Almost everyone has spots at some time or another, and lots of people get greasy hair. It's very common to feel self-conscious about these things, especially when photos all over social media show people who've used digital filters to show themselves with perfect-looking skin.

Everyone's skin produces a kind of oil called sebum. Without it, your skin and hair would dry out. But the huge changes in your hormone levels during puberty, especially in testosterone, can increase sebum production. Result: spots and greasy hair.

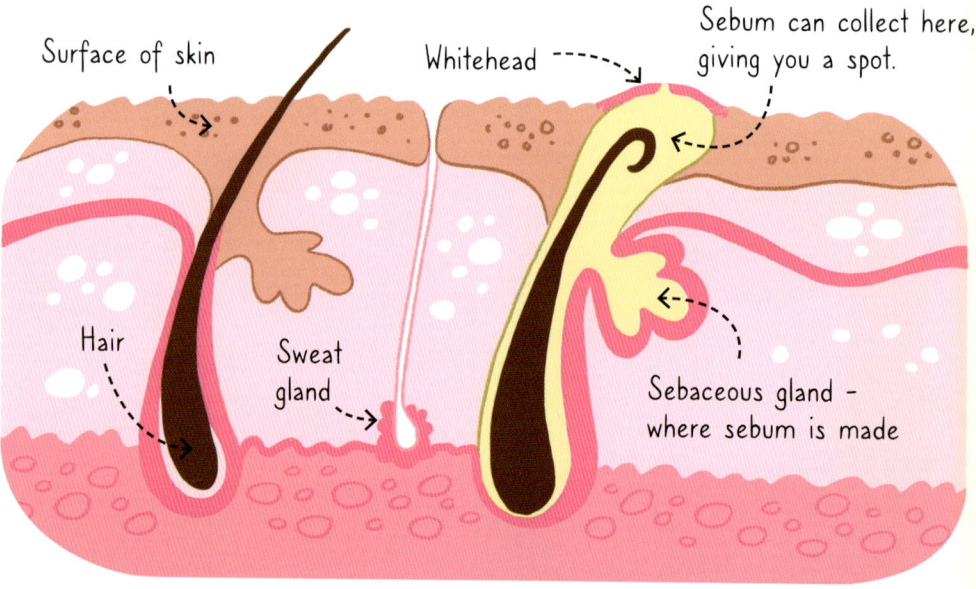

DEALING WITH SPOTS

Different people swear by different spot remedies. The best thing is to find out which works best for you.

Wash your face every day with a mild, unperfumed or antiseptic soap. Use warm water and your bare hands.

Try one of the spot treatments you can buy from a pharmacy.

Use as few beauty products as possible if you're in a spotty phase. Medicated concealer sticks can give good camouflage for just one or two spots.

If you have lots of spots, you don't have to put up with them – ask your pharmacist or doctor what to do.

If you do end up squeezing the odd spot (and it's often really tempting!), there are a few precautions to take.

- Wash your hands first.
- Use your fingers, not your nails.
- Only squeeze blackheads or whiteheads, nothing red or angry.
- Stop if nothing happens, or if clear fluid or blood comes out.
- Dab on an antiseptic, such as tea tree oil, afterwards.
- Wash your hands again.

OLDER AND WISER

One of the fun parts of puberty is gaining your independence. By the time you're grown up, you'll be able to make more decisions and take responsibility for yourself. This is really exciting! But it doesn't mean you can just do whatever you want all the time. You have to keep yourself safe.

CYBER SAFETY

You'll be told over and over again that you need to be safe online – it's boring, but it's true! The internet is an extremely helpful resource, but it comes with some risks. Create strong passwords to keep your accounts private, and don't share your full name, home address or the name of your school online. Before you post or share a photo, remember that you can never be sure who will see, save or forward it on. And most importantly, never chat to someone you don't know.

DRUGS

Drugs are chemicals that change the way your brain and body work, usually for a short time. When people talk about the dangers of drugs, they mostly mean illegal drugs such as ecstasy (a small pill) or cannabis (either a weed people smoke, or sweets they chew, known as "edibles").

But actually the word "drugs" includes other, legal, things that can be addictive and dangerous, such as painkilling medicines and caffeine-heavy energy drinks.

Nicotine (in vapes) and alcohol (in beer, wine or spirits) are all addictive drugs that can be very bad for your health, especially when your body is still developing. It's important to remember that all drugs affect each person differently, so you can never be sure how YOUR body will react to them.

Some people take drugs because they don't want to feel left out, or because they think it will make them look more grown-up. Don't let yourself be pressured to try something just to fit in – it's always okay to say no.

YOUR SUPPORT CREW

Family and friends can be a good source of support to help you through the tricky business of growing up. But, during puberty, it's normal for these relationships to start to feel a bit different too. It's also, sadly, very normal to go through times when you feel lonely, and have to cope with bullies.

AT HOME

As you get older, you'll probably get into occasional arguments with your parents. When parents set rules, it's often because they want the best for you. But it can still feel *very* frustrating when you disagree. Communicating your feelings calmly with the people close to you is a good way to set new boundaries as you mature. This might sound something like...

FRIENDS AND ENEMIES

It's also normal to get into arguments or even fights with your friends. Swirling hormones make for clouded thinking, and it's all too easy to find yourself saying something mean, or even hitting out.

It's never okay to hit people, and it's not nice to hurt someone's feelings. It's not possible to be calm and perfect at all times! You have to learn a new skill – forgiveness. That means, if someone has hurt you – and they are clearly sorry about it – letting go of your own anger. It also means YOU learning to say sorry and ask someone else for their forgiveness, too.

Friends are people who are nice to you even after you've lost your temper, and people *you* can forgive when they've lost their temper, too.

POWER AND RESPONSIBILITY

One of the best parts of growing up is that you get to be physically bigger and stronger. You'll be able to run faster and jump higher than ever before! You'll probably learn to use new words and experiment with jokes.

All these new skills are super exciting, but beware! Your actions have an impact. If you're trading punches in a play fight, or insults in a rap battle, you might hit harder than you intended. Be a hero – look out for the little guy.

FRIENDSHIPS

It's normal for friendship groups to shift around during puberty as people develop new interests and mature at different rates. True friends will value you for who you really are, so you shouldn't feel pressured to change in order to fit in.

You might feel as though everyone is looking at you, or worry about what other people think. Scientists call this an imaginary audience, and everyone experiences it. If you feel self-conscious, it might be helpful to remember that other people are worrying about fitting in too. They most likely don't notice details about you, such as how you look.

ROLE MODELS

As well as friends, you might have role models – people you admire. They might be people you know, such as an older brother or sister, or a teacher, or an athlete or actor or an influencer. It's common for teens to crush on a celebrity, or develop an obsession with them. Making up fantasies about someone you'll never actually meet is a safe way to explore your feelings. But remember that your fantasy of what a person is like is not the same as what they are *really* like.

Just because you admire someone, you don't have to become like them. However much you wish it, you might go through puberty and find that you're not built to be an athlete, or interested in living a rock star lifestyle.

You are, and can only ever be, YOURSELF.

TOO GOOD TO BE TRUE?

You might have seen videos online of people telling you that "real men" drive fast cars, have jobs that make them rich, and have loads of girlfriends or boyfriends. It sounds a lot more fun than going to school and working hard for the rest of your life.

In fact, there's a lot that those videos DON'T talk about. For example, the person on film might well come from a rich family.

Of course they can get whatever they want without working hard – they just buy it. They also don't say if their girlfriends are actually in love with them – or if they're just pretending to look happy on camera. Some even commit crimes to get what they want. If something seems too good to be true, it probably is.

MANLINESS

For many years people have had ideas of what it means to be manly. You might have heard that men shouldn't cry, or show their feelings. Or that they should be strong and mean and always be in charge.

These are outdated gender stereotypes. Men can and should cry, and show any other feelings, too. In fact, you can be WHOEVER you want to be, so long as your choices don't hurt other people. It won't make you less of a man – but it will make you a better, happier person.

Calm

Friendly and approachable

STRONG

Smart

Sporty

FUNNY

Someone who keeps their head down

Someone who thinks things through

Pretty

Quiet

Daring

Someone who looks out for my friends

Obedient

Not afraid to ask for help

Disobedient :)

WHAT KIND OF PERSON DO I WANT TO BE?

Self-sufficient

Someone other people notice

Someone who can see another's point of view

Decisive

Gentle

Generous

Someone who doesn't complain a lot

TOUGH

Determined

Fashionable

Someone who DOES complain, when they see problems

Honest

Someone who tries new things

BECOMING YOU

Discovering who you are takes time, and it's not something that stops after puberty. Your identity will shift and change throughout your life, so you don't need to have everything figured out right away.

Take time to experiment with clothes, listen to different styles of music, try your hand at new hobbies and meet lots of new people.

There will be times when you want to fit in with other people, and worry that you don't. There will be times when you're glad to be different, even if it sometimes makes life tough. There will be plenty of times when you're happy, too.

This is all NORMAL. Now that you know all about your changing body, put this book down and go have some fun.

GLOSSARY

Words in *italic* type are defined in their own entries.

Clitoris Sensitive, pea-shaped bump near the top of the *vulva*
Coming out When a person tells someone else about their *sexuality*
Condom A method of *contraception* that goes over the *penis* to stop *sperm* getting into the *vagina*. Also prevents *STIs* spreading
Consent Asking for permission before touching another person
Contraception Methods used to stop someone getting *pregnant* when *having sex*
Contraceptive pill A method of *contraception* that works by taking a pill each day, often just called "the pill"
Discharge White or milky fluid that keeps the *vagina* clean
Drugs Pills, liquids, powders and gases that temporarily change the way your brain and body feel, often addictive and dangerous
Eggs Tiny parts of the body made in the *ovaries*. Each month, one egg comes out of one ovary. It comes out of the *vagina* as a *period*, unless it fuses with *sperm* to become a baby
Ejaculation When *semen* comes out of the *penis*
Erection When extra blood flows into the *penis*, making it hard or stiff
Gender How a person identifies themself, for example as being male, female, or both, or neither
Gender stereotypes The mistaken idea that some people should act or look a certain way because of their *gender*
Genitals Your private body bits that are in between your legs
Hormones Chemical messages in your blood that tell your body to do different things, such as starting *puberty*
Intersex Someone born with a mix of male and female *sex organs* and *hormones*; often impossible to tell just by looking
Masturbation When someone rubs or touches their own *genitals* in a way that might lead to an *orgasm*
Orgasm A shuddering, happy feeling that people may get when their

genitals are touched or rubbed. It usually lasts a few seconds, also known as "coming"

Ovaries Part of the female *sex organs* where *eggs* are stored

Penis Part of the male *genitals* that hangs down in between the legs

Period A time when the lining of the *womb* comes out of the *vagina* as period blood for a few days each month

Period products Things girls can use to soak up *period* blood, such as tampons, pads, cups and period pants

PMS (Premenstrual syndrome) Feeling sad, irritated or anxious in the days leading up to a *period*

Pornography Grown-up videos or images of people being naked, *having sex*, or touching each other's private body bits

Pregnancy When a *sperm* fuses with an *egg* which causes a baby to start growing in the *womb*

Puberty When the body starts making lots of new *hormones* that bring about growing-up changes

Semen A white, gooey fluid containing *sperm* that can come out of the *penis* during *ejaculation*

Sex The word sex is used to mean two different things:
- **1.** The body bits a person is born with – typically female, male or intersex.
- **2.** "Having sex" is when people touch each other's *genitals* in a way that might make an *orgasm* happen.

Sex organs Parts of the body related to *having sex* and making babies

Sexuality A word used to describe either the type of people you're attracted to, or that you don't feel attracted to anyone

Sperm Tiny body parts found in *semen* that can lead to a baby being made, if one of them fuses with an *egg*

Testicles Part of the male *sex organs* where *sperm* is made

Vagina The opening to a tube inside a female body where *discharge* and *period* blood comes out

Vulva The name for the female body bits between the legs

Wet dream A dream that may lead to an *orgasm* during sleep

Womb (uterus) Part of the female *sex organs* where a baby can grow

INDEX

babies, 28, 35
beards, 12-13
brain, 6, 40
breasts, 28-29
bullying, 53

clitoris, 24-25
coming out, 31
consent, 32-33, 35
contraception, 36-37

drugs, 57

eggs, 26, 35
ejaculation, 16, 17, 18, 35
emotions, 7, 40, 53
erections, 15-16, 18-19
exercise, 44-45

food, 42-43
foreskin, 14, 15, 47

gender, 20-23, 30
gender stereotypes, 22, 56
girls, 13, 24-29
growth spurt, 8

hair, 10-13
hormones, 6-7, 26, 53

infections, 36, 37
intersex, 21, 23

manliness, 56-57

masturbation, 16-17
muscles, 9, 53

orgasms, 16, 25, 34
ovaries, 26

penis, 14-16, 35, 36
periods, 26-27, 36
period products, 27
PMS, 27
pornography, 38-39
pregnancy, 36, 37
puberty, 3-6
pubic hair, 10, 13, 25

safe sex, 36-37
semen, 16-17, 35
sex, 33, 34-37, 38-39
sex and gender, 20-23, 30-31
sexuality, 30-31
shaving, 12
sleep, 45
smegma, 47
sperm, 16, 35
spots, 48-49
stereotypes, 22, 56-57
STIs, 37

testicles, 6, 7, 14, 16

vagina, 24, 25, 26-27, 35
voice breaking, 9
vulva, 24-25

wet dreams, 18

MORE INFORMATION

There's a lot to say about growing up, and we couldn't fit absolutely everything into one book.
At **Usborne Quicklinks**, you can find links to websites with more facts about puberty and the changes that happen as you grow. You can also find links to organizations that offer support, advice, and answers to questions you might have about topics in the book.

To get started, scan the code, or go to usborne.com/Quicklinks and type in the title of this book.

Usborne Publishing is not responsible for the content of external websites. Children should be supervised online. Please follow the online safety guidelines at **usborne.com/Quicklinks**

ACKNOWLEDGEMENTS

EDITOR: Jane Chisholm
COVER DESIGNER: Anna Gould
SERIES DESIGNER: Zoe Wray

EXPERT CONSULTANTS:
Dr Anna Forringer-Beal, University of Cambridge Centre for Gender Studies
Dr Caitríona Cox, Addenbrooke's Hospital (Cambridge University Hospitals Trust)
Laura Clarke, sex educator

WITH SPECIAL THANKS TO
Alice James, Darran Stobbart, Micaela Tapsell, Amy Chiu,
Ashe de Sousa, Stefanie Felsberger...

...and the many, *many* people who read the book
and suggested ways to make it more inclusive,
more relevant, and more fun!

First published in 2025 by Usborne Publishing Limited,
83–85 Saffron Hill, London EC1N 8RT, United Kingdom.
usborne.com

Copyright © 2025 Usborne Publishing Limited. The name Usborne and the Balloon logo are registered trade marks of Usborne Publishing Limited. All rights reserved. No part of this publication may be reproduced or used in any manner for the purpose of training artificial intelligence technologies or systems (including for text or data mining), stored in a retrieval system or transmitted in any form or by any means without the prior permission of the publisher. UKE.